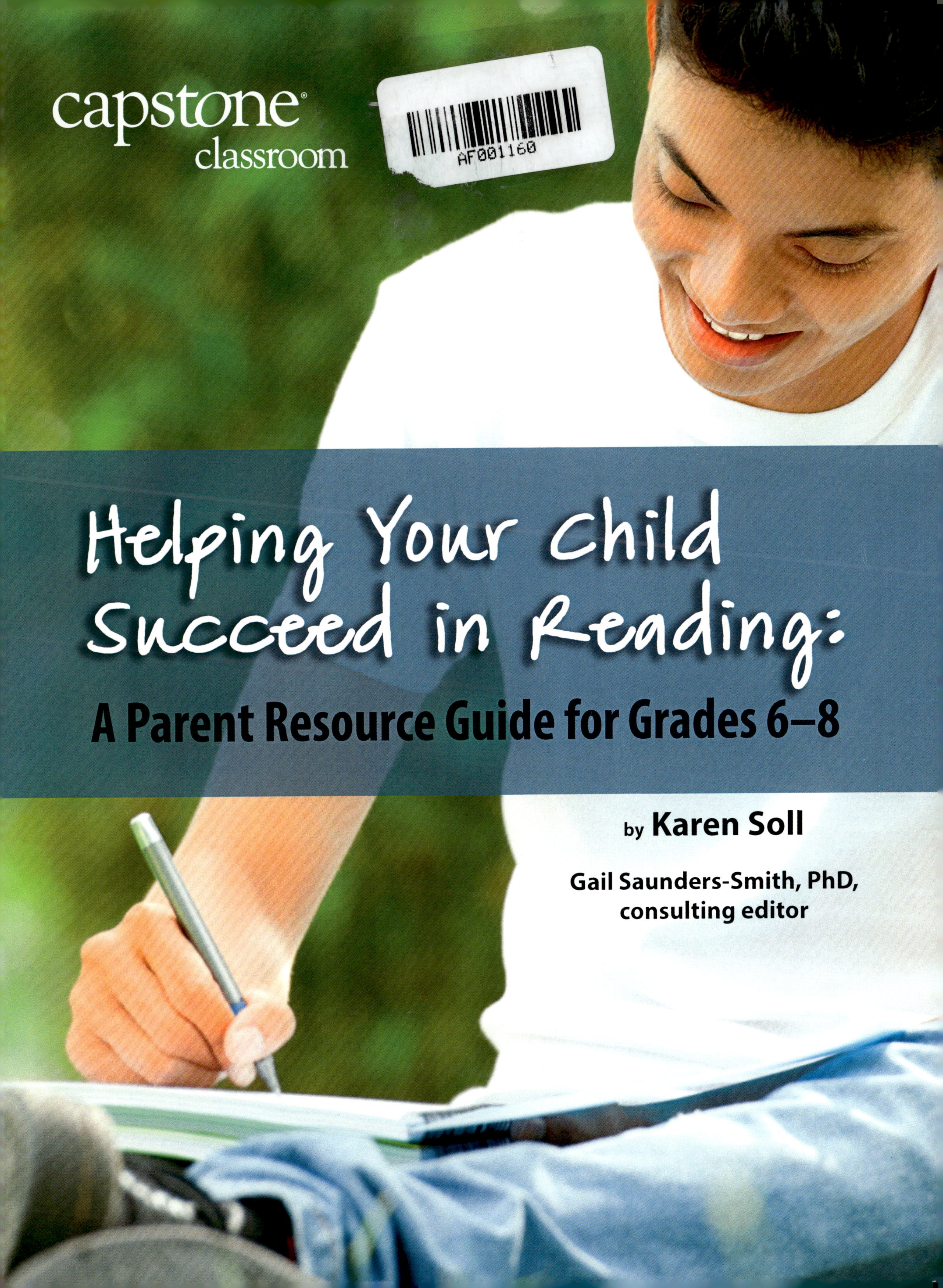

Helping Your Child Succeed in Reading:
A Parent Resource Guide for Grades 6–8

by **Karen Soll**

Gail Saunders-Smith, PhD,
consulting editor

capstone® classroom

Introduction

You are your child's first teacher. You taught your child how to walk, how to talk, and maybe even how to ride a bicycle. The bond you have with your child is like no other. Reading to your child not only strengthens that bond but it also keeps the learning alive while reinforcing the skills taught at school.

You may be wondering how a simple activity such as reading aloud to your child could reinforce skills. If you think about it, you are encouraging a love of reading as you use different voices while reading the *Harry Potter* series to your child. Your child is on the edge of his or her seat, wondering what's going to happen next to the young boy.

If you're wondering what else you can do to enhance reading skills, here are some easy-to-implement routines. So get cozy and feel free to adapt the activities according to your child's stage of development.

Where to Begin

A lot of research says the more time your child spends reading, the more he or she will be able to read different types of books of varying complexity. Reading books published by Capstone is a start.

Then reinforce skills learned in school while reading together. Discuss the meaning of an unfamiliar word, or help answer questions your child may have. You can also provide supplementary information about a historical event or make a connection to other events. You can be detectives, figuring out answers that might not be in the book or make connections to other things your child has seen or read. These are skills that your child is doing in school every day, and they are activities you can do while enjoying a book together.

Use this resource as a tool while reading with your child. It includes helpful tips, strategies, and activities. They're easy to do and can be added to your normal routine. And, of course, they can be achieved with any book on your shelf. We suggest that you review the tips with your child's development in mind to make the most of this special time together.

Tips for Grades 6-8

Your child knows whether he or she likes to read. Help build a love of reading while also reinforcing some of the work that's being done by your child's teacher. At these grade levels, your child is being asked to:

- question,
- make inferences,
- draw conclusions,
- write responses,
- answer comprehension questions,
- share evidence,
- probe deeper,
- paraphrase and summarize, and
- connect the book to other books or real life.

While reading aloud to your child, take the time to enjoy the book, and see whether your child understands what is being read. Here are just a few activities you could do with your child.

- Give your child choice in which book will be read. If your child is unable to make a decision, show your child two to three books and allow him or her to choose the book.

- Stop every now and then to ask your child a question. You can ask such questions as, "What do you think it means to … ," "Why do you think she behaved that way?," or "What would you do?" These types of questions get at the heart of the book, and encourage your child to think deeply about the content.

- You may run across a word or phrase that your child does not know. Prompt him or her to use the clues in the sentence, paragraph, or picture (called context clues) to figure out what it means.

- Allow your child to stop the reading to ask questions. If the answer may be found in the text, ask your child to try to find it.

- Use an engaging voice, and read the different parts of the book in a different way. To build tension, read a part slowly or in a whisper, and slowly turn the page.

- Sometimes, the author does not include all the information in book. He or she may leave something out on purpose or leave a gap for the reader to fill in. You can help your child fill in these gaps by asking him or her questions about them, such as, "What do we know about the character that would lead him to act the way he does?" Filling in these gaps will help your child make a deeper connection to what has been read. Also use this time to ask whether the author did a good job of giving information. This encourages your child to think critically about the book and the author's work.

- Ask your child to make a connection between the book you read and another book that is similar. For example, if you read a book together about panda bears, you can ask your child if there was another book he or she read about animals in China. You can also connect this to his or her world by asking about a TV show or a trip to the zoo.

- After you read the book, ask your child to retell the events. Also ask if he or she liked the book. This gives you a good gauge on the types of materials to read for next time.

Tips for Developing Readers

Developing readers are children who are continuing to develop their reading skills. Some children can pick up their favorite book and plow right through it. They are motivated to read because the book is on a subject that is near and dear to their hearts. And yet, give them a book about something else and they may struggle to understand what that book is about. They may not have enough background knowledge about the topic in order to fully understand the book. Perhaps the book is filled with vocabulary that is unfamiliar, making the book a frustrating read.

Of course, these kinds of books include information that is good to know. Help your child build his or her reading muscles accordingly.

- Always encourage choice. It may help to show your child a few books, and have him or her select the book.

- Show your child the book title and picture on the front cover. We suggest telling your child what the book is about and then engaging in a conversation on what he or she already knows about the subject.

- Without reading the book, turn each page, and talk through each picture. If you see a word in bold on the page, use that word when describing the pictures. Gauge at this time whether your child understands the vocabulary.

- Read the book, and encourage your child to ask questions about anything that he or she doesn't understand. Spend some time discussing the answers.

- If your child seems eager to do so, let him or her read a page you are on. Ask your child how the pictures might connect to the passage. Pay attention to whether your child struggles when reading any of the words. Writing sentences with these words on flashcards for practice later on will help him or her.

- Show your child graphic organizers like diagrams and charts. Explain that these features reinforce what the book is about. They often add a little more information too. Read the features together and ask your child what it added to the book.

- After reading the book, ask your child what is something new that he or she learned. If your child has a question about the book, do some supplementary research on the topic online to see whether there is more information that can be found.

capstone
classroom

1710 Roe Crest Drive,
North Mankato, Minnesota 56003
www.capstoneclassroom.com

Copyright © 2015 by Capstone Classroom, a division of Capstone. All rights reserved. No part of this publication may be reproduced in whole or in part, or stored in a retrieval system, or transmitted in any form or by any means, electronic, mechanical, photocopying, recording, or otherwise, without written permission of the publisher. For information regarding permission, write to Capstone Classroom, 1710 Roe Crest Drive, North Mankato, Minnesota 56003.

Helping Your Child Succeed in Reading: A Parent Resource Guide for Grades 6–8

978-1-62521-956-5

About the Author: Karen Soll has a M.Ed. in curriculum and instruction, and several years experience working on a variety of core and supplemental materials for the education market.

Printed in the United States of America in Eau Claire, Wisconsin.
052620   003523